Original title:
Green Therapy

Copyright © 2025 Creative Arts Management OÜ
All rights reserved.

Author: Thomas Sinclair
ISBN HARDBACK: 978-1-80581-755-0
ISBN PAPERBACK: 978-1-80581-282-1
ISBN EBOOK: 978-1-80581-755-0

Fragrance of the Forest

In the wood, a scent that sways,
A skunk's lost socks on sunny days.
The pine trees sneeze, and leaves conspire,
To play the tune of forest choir.

Mushrooms dance, with polka dots,
Squirrels hoard forgotten thoughts.
The brook giggles, splashes about,
While puzzled frogs jump all about.

Resilience in Roots

A weed pokes up through cracked concrete,
Winking at cars with scrappy feet.
Its leafy grin, a bold surprise,
Saying, "Look at me! I rise!"

While flowers in the garden pout,
This tough one makes a raucous shout.
With roots like rubber bands, it sings,
Unbothered by the snipping things.

Echoing the Earth's Heart

The ground goes thump, the trees hum back,
A dance of earth beneath the crack.
Ants march in a parade so sweet,
Offering crumbs for the beetle fleet.

Rabbits wear hats made out of grass,
While gophers gossip as they pass.
The earth's heartbeat, a funny tune,
In a soil concert under the moon!

A Song of Blooms

The daisies cheer, in yellow caps,
While tulips sing of garden naps.
Marigolds giggle, dressed in gold,
Tickling bees, both brave and bold.

A lily twirls, a simple prank,
Splashing dew upon the bank.
With every puff, a petal flies,
In a floral dance beneath the skies!

Solitude in the Grove

In the woods, I lost my shoes,
The squirrels stole them, what a ruse!
I tripped on roots, fell down with flair,
The trees just laughed, they didn't care.

Whispers of wind through branches swayed,
Critters chuckled as I prayed.
The mushrooms giggled, quite the sight,
I joined their dance, it felt so right.

Beneath the Boughs

A rabbit hops by wearing shades,
Cooler than me, I'm lost in spades.
The sun peeks in, a playful tease,
As I try to nap with buzzing bees.

The leaves above have started to chatter,
About my style, which doesn't matter.
I wink at the squirrels pretending to car,
Who knew nature had such comedic stars?

Emerald Serenity

I found a bench draped in moss,
Sat down for peace, and what a toss!
A deer beside me, trying to chat,
About life choices—my past was fat!

The frogs joined in with a croak and leap,
"Relax!" they said, "there's no need to weep!"
I laughed so hard, my worries flew,
Nature's therapy, who knew it too?

The Language of the Forest

The trees were speaking, oh what a twist,
I caught their gossip, couldn't resist.
"Did you see the guy scaring the bug?"
"Yeah, I heard, it made me shrug!"

Beneath the boughs, life's not so dull,
With chirpy birds calling in a lull.
They mocked my style, my sunburned nose,
Nature's humor, I suppose it grows!

Light through the Leaves

Sunlight dances on high,
Leaves giggle as they sway,
A breeze whispers a lie,
'We're trees, not here to play!'

A squirrel swings by, oh dear,
My hat flies off with a shout,
Frogs croak laughter, how queer,
Nature's jesters all about!

A rabbit hops in a blink,
Carrots tucked in its cheek,
While I just stop and think,
In this chaos, I feel sleek!

The sun waves goodbye,
As shadows start to creep,
With leaves as my ally,
I'll chuckle myself to sleep!

Renewal by the River

The river sings a song,
Throwing jokes like stones,
Its current's humor strong,
Tickling tired old bones.

Otters slide with a splash,
Cartwheeling with delight,
While I'm just trying to dash,
To avoid a soggy plight!

Moss grows thick like a beard,
On rocks that seem to grin,
Nature's puns are well-heard,
As birds join in the din.

The sun sets, casting gold,
As laughter drifts away,
In this world, young and old,
Find joy in nature's play!

Guided by the Green

The path beneath my feet,
Is lined with laughs galore,
Where flowers and weeds meet,
They poke fun, then implore.

The bees buzz with a roar,
Dancers in puffy suits,
While I trip, then explore,
Chasing those buzzing brutes!

Pine trees whisper secrets,
"Why can't you climb a wall?"
I shrug; they have their fetes,
But I just keep the thrall!

The grass tickles my toes,
As I lie there and dream,
In this world, joy just grows,
In nature's funny scheme!

Meadow Meditation

In a field, I take pause,
Daisies start their debate,
"Why do we have no claws?"
"Because that would be great!"

I chuckle at their fight,
As butterflies flutter by,
A dance in pure delight,
While I give yoga a try!

The clouds form silly shapes,
A hippo doing the twist,
As the sun playfully drapes,
A smile I can't resist.

Resting among the blooms,
With laughter all around,
Nature's humor resumes,
In this joy I am found!

Abiding Harmony in Green

In the garden where weeds twist and twirl,
Life's little quirks start to unfurl.
A snail in a race, oh what a sight,
Taking its time, while others take flight.

The sunbeams laugh on the patchy grass,
As ants throw a party, oh what a class!
With daisies peeking in delight,
They dance all day, into the night.

Birds tweet gossip, with a side of cheer,
About the squirrel who lost its rear.
Leaves wear hats made of dew and lace,
In this leafy realm, it's a comical place.

In the quiet shade, the laughter sounds,
As nature reveals its playful bounds.
So if you seek joy, just give a glance,
Nature, my friend, throws the best dance.

The Dance of the Dandelions

Dandelions waltz on a breeze so spry,
With fluffy white hats that whisper and sigh.
They giggle and jiggle while dodging the bees,
A party of petals that wave in the breeze.

With roots set in mischief, they sprout with a grin,
Who knew such trouble could start with a spin?
They sprout in the cracks, oh so bold and spry,
Claiming the sidewalk, those rebels defy.

Look out for the clover, it's plotting a show,
It's bringing the luck, with a dash of glow.
While butterflies twirl in their colorful chase,
In this garden of laughter, we all find our place.

So here's to the dandelions, wild and free,
The jesters of nature, come join their jubilee.
With smiles that stretch wide, they root and they play,
Reminding us all to laugh every day.

Cradled in the Canopy

Underneath leaves that giggle and sway,
The squirrels hold court, laugh at their play.
With acorns for hats, they strut with such glee,
In this woodland kingdom, all wild and free.

Branches are stages for sprites on parade,
Swinging from tendrils, in shadows they wade.
A raccoon's a joker, flipping through snacks,
As twigs snapping 'round sound like wild little cracks.

The sunlight spills in with a bright, golden grin,
The trees tell their secrets to all who come in.
As laughter erupts from the ferns on the floor,
Nature's a comedian, with jokes to explore.

So when you feel weary, take shelter in green,
Let the rustle of leaves be the best kind of scene.
With friends made of branches and laughter so sweet,
In a canopy cradle, all troubles retreat.

Nature's Quiet Prayer

In the garden, worms hold court,
With dirt pies and their snails consort.
The daisies giggle, swaying wide,
While ants march by, their chins held high.

Bees buzzing jokes, oh what a buzz!
A flower snickers, it surely does.
The trees gossip, leaves swish and sway,
Nature's laughter brightening the day.

The Calm of the Cosmos

Stars in the sky, they play peek-a-boo,
As planets dance, in a cosmic zoo.
A comet sneezes, oh what a show!
While aliens chuckle, 'Let's steal the glow!'

Galaxies whirling, a dizzying spree,
Satellites whisper, 'Did you just see?'
Asteroids tumble, with grace and flair,
Space is a circus, beyond compare!

Awakened by the Elements

Sun wakes the flowers, a tickle or two,
While raindrops fall, and dance on the dew.
Wind tells a story, in a silly voice,
And thunder replies, 'Hey, don't make me hoist!'

Fireflies flicker, like lanterns afloat,
While the sun pretends, it's wearing a coat.
Mountains chuckle, with pebbles that grin,
Nature's a jester, inviting us in.

Leafy Soliloquy

A leaf on the ground tells tales of the breeze,
'Oh my, what a ride! It was all just a tease!'
Trees shimmy and shake, sharing silly tricks,
While squirrels join in, with their nutty antics.

Moss softly giggles, feeling quite grand,
As mushrooms play chess, in their little band.
Vines twist and twirl, with a whimsical cheer,
In this leafy realm, there's laughter to hear.

Sanctuary of the Spirit

In the garden where gnomes play,
A raccoon steals my sandwich away.
I laugh as the lilies start to sway,
Nature's jest, brightening my day.

The daffodils giggle in the breeze,
While squirrels are plotting, if you please.
They whisper tales from towering trees,
Oh, come join this frolic with such ease!

A turtle sunbathes on a rock,
I think he's auditioning for a sock.
He strikes a pose, he'll never clock,
What joy this critter brings to my block!

With butterflies dancing, all in sync,
And a toad croaking his thoughts, I think,
This green haven with its cheerful link,
In nature's punchline, I find my wink.

A Tapestry of Green

In the park where the daisies sprout,
A parrot squawks, adding to the clout.
I declare, in my sunhat and pout,
This nature's a stage, there's never a doubt.

The trees wear scarves made of vine,
Whispering secrets in a line.
I can hear them argue about the wine,
As squirrels join in for a quick feline.

A frog leaps high, aiming for the snack,
Missing the flies and landing with a whack.
Laughter erupts, no virtue to track,
This symphony of green is pure knack.

With daisies dancing, a comedic show,
The sun smiles wide, seemingly aglow.
In this patch of laughter, feelings flow,
A tapestry of humor starts to grow.

Soft Echoes of the Grove

In the grove where shadows play tricks,
A hedgehog attempts a few magic flicks.
With acorns rolling and nature's picks,
Laughter rings as he flops and kicks.

The owls hoot jokes in starlit chatter,
While rabbits munch on dandelion splatter.
In this forest, nothing's the matter,
We giggle as the leaves start to clatter.

A wise old tree joins in the jest,
With roots that tickle, it's not a test.
As branches sway, feeling quite blessed,
In soft echoes, we find our rest.

With crickets scoring our nightly play,
Nature's theatre, a grand array.
Each rustle and whisper leads the way,
To soft echoes that make us sway.

Mending with Moss

On a log where the moss grows thick,
A snail finds refuge, taking his pick.
With a slow-mo race, what a quirky trick,
Life's vibrant mosaic, all nature's click.

When the ferns start to gossip aloud,
And the fungi throw a leafy crowd,
I join the fun, feeling quite proud,
In this earthy dance, wrapped like a shroud.

The sunbeams tap-dance on damp stones,
While a lost sock lies in nature's loans.
Mending with moss, laughing with tones,
In a woodland world where nothing's too prone.

With every giggle, a petal will bloom,
This therapy blooms, dispelling all gloom.
Amongst the green, we find our room,
Mending with moss, dispelling the doom.

Whispers of the Leaf

In the breeze, the leaves chuckle,
As squirrels plot their next big struggle.
Grass blades gossip, soft and low,
While flowers dance in a silly show.

A bird drops a joke, just for fun,
While bees buzz in, saying, "We're not done!"
The sun joins in, with a wink so bright,
Nature's comedy, pure delight!

Nature's Embrace

When mushrooms wear hats, oh what a sight,
Frogs in tuxedos croak with delight.
The wind tells stories of silly antics,
While ants march by, wearing their antics.

Butterflies giggle, flitting by,
With dragonflies buzzing, oh me, oh my!
Nature's embrace, a laughter spree,
Where every creature joins in a glee!

The Healing Canopy

Under the canopy, leaves perform tricks,
As branches sway, sharing their picks.
A raccoon sneezes, and everyone laughs,
While the owl gives side-eyes, calculating gaffs.

Sunlight plays peek-a-boo through the trees,
The shadows giggle, feeling the breeze.
Each rustle a laugh, every sound a cheer,
Nature's giggle—it's perfectly clear!

Breaths of the Earth

When daisies blow kisses, and tulips blush,
A hedgehog wiggles in a playful rush.
The earth takes a breath, with a whoosh and a sigh,
As clouds dress up, looking spry in the sky.

Worms throw a party, down in the dirt,
With earthworms dancing, no need for a skirt!
Laughter erupts from each little nook,
Nature's joyous story, come take a look!

Whispering Willows

Willows wave as if they know,
Tickling toes and making glow.
They whisper secrets, soft and sly,
While squirrels plot their acorn pie.

A breeze comes by with winks and nods,
The flowers laugh, the grass just nods.
A dance of leaves, a twist, a twirl,
Nature's jesters, in a whirl.

A honeybee in tiny jeans,
Buzzing around, living dreams.
He flirts with blooms, oh what a scene,
In gardens bright and evergreen.

So, let's all sway with nature's tune,
And skip through fields beneath the moon.
With chuckles shared, let's sip and sip,
Sweet nectar of life, let's take a trip.

Nature's Gentle Hand

Nature's hand is soft and sweet,
With gentle nudges, oh what a treat!
It whispers, "Hey, come take a stroll,"
While frogs croak out their funny role.

Sunbeams tickle grassy plains,
While butterflies play silly games.
The daisies giggle in the breeze,
A lively joke among the trees.

Bumblebees wear tiny hats,
They buzz about like charming frats.
And ants parade in perfect lines,
Declaring, "We've got snacks, just dine!"

A swaying branch invites a dance,
While nature gives us all a chance.
To laugh with leaves, to play pretend,
In every whisper, joy transcends.

Life beneath the Oak

Beneath the oak, the critters meet,
With furry friends, oh what a feat!
They share their snacks, acorns and cheese,
And giggle softly in the breeze.

A chipmunk's prank sends sparks of laughter,
While worms plot out their hidden chapter.
The light above twinkles, just for fun,
As shadows stretch, they say, "We've won!"

Squirrels show off their acrobatics,
With hops and jumps, all elastic.
The whole oak tree joins the show,
Rustling leaves, a real-life pro!

So gather close, forget your fuss,
In nature's realm, it's all robust.
With laughter shared beneath the oak,
Join in the fun, that's no mere joke!

Inhale the Essence of Earth

Breathe in deep, oh what a treat,
The smell of grass, oh isn't it sweet?
Flavors of mint, and daisies bloom,
Nature's perfume fills every room.

The clouds roll by, they're quite the jest,
Wearing shapes that tease the best.
A dragon there, a cat on high,
Watch them play in the open sky.

The rivers giggle, talking fast,
While fish make faces as they pass.
Each drop a joke, a punchline spun,
In nature's laughter, we have fun.

So close your eyes, let senses flow,
Inhale the joy, let good vibes grow.
With nature's humor, life's a game,
Just take a breath, let's stake our claim!

Verdant Reflections

In a garden of lettuce and kale,
I once tried to take a snail.
But it turned out to be my shoe,
Stuck on my foot, what a view!

Tomatoes giggle, roots in a race,
Carrots compete for the best hiding space.
I swear they laugh when I bend down,
To pick them up, wearing a crown!

Grass tickles toes, making me squeal,
While flowers gossip about my zeal.
One bloom whispered, 'A wig, how bold!'
'Twirl, darling, let your hair unfold!'

Honeybees buzzing, a brand new beat,
Doing the cha-cha on dainty feet.
I joined in the fun, but oh what a sight,
A dance-off with ants, a true delight!

Blooming Resilience

A daisy tied a bow and said,
'With my bright petals, all fears are shed!'
But I tripped on a weed in my dance,
Knocked over by a clumsy plant's prance.

Sunflowers flaunt their brilliant hues,
'Call us if you need some good news!'
But when I asked for a little cheer,
They just laughed and waved, 'Not here, dear!'

Cacti gave me a prickly embrace,
Said, 'Survive! Just keep up the pace!'
But when I arrived, they took one look,
And said, 'You're not prickly—just a fluke!'

Then tulips whispered sweetly, 'Oh please,
Worry less, relax in the breeze!'
So I flopped on the grass, with giggles galore,
And soon found my worries were gone for sure.

The Calm of the Woods

In the woods where the squirrels play,
I thought I'd spend the whole day.
But I slipped on an acorn, oh what a fall!
The trees roared with laughter, I heard them all!

A rabbit hopped by, wearing a tie,
'Life's more fun when you aim for the sky!'
I tried to be cool with my very best pose,
But ended up posing like a fallen rose!

Leaves whispered secrets, their giggles did float,
'The pine cone is dating the old oak, we note!'
But I tripped over roots, my face turned a shade,
And suddenly, it felt like a charade!

As shadows danced in the fading light,
I found myself chuckling, feeling just right.
So I embraced the quirk of the woodsy spree,
Turns out nature's comedy is good company!

Echoes of Spring

In springtime's jest, the flowers tease,
'We grow so tall, just check with the bees!'
But I sneezed at their pollen, oh what a sight,
A floral confetti, a colorful flight!

Butterflies twirled in a skirt made of grace,
While frogs croaked jokes, hopping out of place.
I joined in their laughter, a chorus so grand,
Stumbling to join the springtime band!

Birds chirped tales of adventurous dreams,
While ants marched in lines with their culinary schemes.
I tried to keep up, but ended on my back,
'Nature's chaotic!' I exclaimed with a crack.

And as the sun dipped low, painting the sky,
I found fun in the flutters, laughter on high.
So here's to spring's whimsical quirks so fine,
Where joy is a blossom, and we're all intertwined!

In the Shade of Trickling Streams

Under the trees, where the shadows play,
Sipping sweet lemonade, oh what a day!
A duck in a tie, he swims with such grace,
While I munch on sandwiches, crumbs on my face.

A frog in a hat croaks a tune so loud,
Ribbiting rhymes, he's drawing a crowd.
The bugs all are dancing, in miniature shoes,
Nature's own party, we've got nothing to lose.

The breeze gives a tickle, my hair's a wild mess,
I laugh at the chaos, I must confess.
The stream giggles softly, it's caught in the fun,
While I splash around, feeling light as a bun.

We plop down on blankets, it's time for a snooze,
With dreams of tomato soup, and fresh, warm bread to use.
Nature's the jester, in this grand show of ours,
Where laughter blooms bright, like the prettiest flowers.

Vibrance in the Garden

In the garden where veggies play hide and seek,
Tomatoes in sunglasses, looking quite chic.
Zucchini throws parties, the carrots all cheer,
While the peas in their pods nap without any fear.

Radishes gossip, they're such little snobs,
While broccoli flexes, the muscle that robs.
The daisies are laughing, they tickle the air,
As butterflies prance without a single care.

Sunflowers giggle with their heads held high,
Waving to bees as they buzz on by.
The lettuce is quipping, "I'm feeling quite green,"
While the radishes say, "We're all part of the scene."

As the sun sets low, the show's in full swing,
A dance of the veggies, oh what joy they bring.
In the bloom of this garden, life's silly yet bright,
With laughter and colors, it's pure, sheer delight.

The Touch of Grass

The grass is a carpet, oh so soft and lush,
A tickle beneath, it makes me hush.
I roll like a tumbleweed, laughing with glee,
While ants throw a party, just under my knee.

My picnic blanket says, "What's this ruckus, my friend?"
While squirrels jump in, looking to blend.
"Is there room for a pebble?" one cheeky rock asks,
While I munch on crackers, behind little grass masks.

Sticky fingers from berries, my face is a sight,
With jammed-up delight, I'm a sticky ball of light.
The lawn gnomes are judging, they think I'm a fool,
But I'm just here basking, making my own rule.

So, here's to the grasses, that cradle my dreams,
In this whimsical world, or so it seems.
With laughter as my guide, I'll frolic and prance,
In the funny embrace of this green, grassy dance.

Nourishment from Nature

A squirrel steals my sandwich, oh what a thief,
Coming down with chirps, it's a moment of grief.
While the apple tree chuckles, "Don't take it too hard,
I've got plenty of fruit; hold your own backyard!"

The berries are squished, in a wild jam concoct,
While grapes form a circus, with breadcrumbs to flock.
"Look at us juggling!" they giggle and sway,
Nature's wholesome buffet, let's feast for the day.

I chew on my greens, without any fuss,
While the radishes wink, "Join us, it's a must!"
In a scrumptious parade of flowers and roots,
We're all taking part in this nutty old hoot.

As laughter erupts, we're all having fun,
Nature's own kitchen, a feast for everyone.
So here's to the madness, the joy it will bring,
Life's silly banquet, let's all dance and sing!

Serenade of Sprouts

In a garden of lettuce, oh what a sight,
Tomatoes are giggling, it's sheer delight.
Carrots are dancing, with tops in the air,
While radishes snicker; they don't have a care.

A snap pea sings out, 'I'm sweet and I'm bold!'
While broccoli boasts of its crown made of gold.
Rabbits hop by, looking curious and smug,
As flowers whisper secrets to the nearest bug.

Cucumbers chuckle, with skin oh so neat,
And onions are crying, but they can't feel the heat.
The earthworms are wriggling, doing a jig,
Saying, 'We're the life of this soil, so big!'

So gather your veggies, let's throw a feast,
Join this merry party, to say the least.
With laughter and joy, we'll relish the plot,
In this whimsical world, there's happiness a lot!

Sylvan Solace

In the dappled woods where the squirrels chase tails,
Fungi concoct their own herbal gales.
Birds chirp in chorus, in suits made of fluff,
While chipmunks declare, 'We've had quite enough!'

Trees gossip to breezes, sharing their woes,
As pollen drifts lazily, tickling your nose.
A deer struts in style, wearing moss as a hat,
While frogs leap in rhythm, like a lively chat.

The streams bubble laughter, so carefree and bright,
As fish play hide-and-seek, what a glorious sight!
Sunbeams paint sparkles on leaves up above,
Nature's odd antics are truly a love.

With picnic baskets full, we'll laugh 'til we drop,
In this realm of green giggles, we won't ever stop.
So let's toast to the woods, with a glass of fresh air,
For sanity found in these moments we share!

Renewal in the Meadow

In a meadow of wonder, where daisies grow tall,
The butterflies giggle, they know it all.
Bees buzz in laughter, working away,
While grasshoppers joke that it's a holiday.

The daisies make crowns, so regal and bright,
While crickets create music under starlight.
The cows munch their cud, with a wink and a nod,
Saying, 'We uplift each other; nature's our god!'

The sun smiles down on this colorful scene,
While wind whispers softly, 'You all are so keen.'
With splashes of color, wildflowers prance,
Join in this wild, whimsical dance!

So gather your friends, laugh, sing, and play,
In the heart of the meadow, where joy leads the way.
For in this mild madness, we find our reprieve,
With each little chuckle, we truly believe!

Gardens of Tranquility

In gardens of laughter, where herbs grow with glee,
Thyme's telling tales, 'Come and listen to me!'
Chives are all snickering at garlic's strong breath,
While basil is planning its next playful theft.

The peas form a line, for a game of charades,
While lettuce rolls over, insisting it fades.
Cilantro's in costume—a leaf on a spree,
While the radishes roll for a dance on the lea.

A scarecrow wears sunglasses, looking quite cool,
He's the reigning champ of the garden school.
The sunflowers sway, in their tall, noble grace,
While butterflies flutter, just chasing a race.

So let's frolic and play, in this magical patch,
With earth's little wonders, we'll find a perfect match.
In laughter and joy, let your spirit unwind,
For peace is this garden, where smiles are entwined!

Blossoms of Joy

In the garden, I take my seat,
Weeds dance 'round me, oh what a treat!
A snail speeds by, trying to win,
I cheer him on, with a goofy grin.

Sunflowers laugh; they're so tall and bright,
They tickle my chin in the morning light.
Petunias gossip, petals a-flutter,
They make me giggle, it's like a stutter!

When bees do the cha-cha on petals so sweet,
I join the dance, can't stay in my seat!
The daisies roll their eyes in delight,
As I twist and shout, what a silly sight!

So here's to the blooms in joyful array,
They whisper laughter, come dance, come play!
In this patch of wonder, I lose my cares,
Nature's a jester, with chuckles it shares!

Sanctuary of Shadows

In a forest deep, where the secrets creep,
I trip on roots, making a heap!
Trees crouch low, like they're plotting a prank,
And squirrels giggle as they stare at my flank.

Mushrooms peek out, with caps so round,
Like little umbrellas, just waiting around.
The shadows gather, they pull me in,
I swear I heard one say, 'Where have you been?'

Branches wave like they're saying hello,
While I bump a bush, and it starts to grow!
The whispers of leaves—oh, they sound just like chat,
They tease me warmly, 'Where's your top hat?'

In this playful nook, time takes a break,
I chuckle with owls, oh what a mistake!
The sanctuary blooms with laughter galore,
Who knew the forest had jokes at its core?

Fern Fragments

Tiny fronds wiggle in the breeze,
They're throwing a party, come join if you please!
With each sway and twist, they've got moves,
Inviting the beetles to show off their grooves.

A ladybug stumbles and falls on her back,
The ferns giggle softly, 'Hey, cut her some slack!'
With soil as the dance floor, and roots as their beat,
Even the worms can't resist tapping their feet!

The sunlight filters through, like a silly hat,
Casting funny shadows of a dancing cat.
In this spot of green, I'm just part of the fun,
Celebrating like it's always a pun!

So come join the ferns, in their whimsical play,
They'll tickle your toes, chase your woes away!
Nature's own laughter, woven in leaves,
In moments of joy, the good heart believes!

Embracing the Earth

Crawling on grass, I've sunk to the ground,
Hugging a worm who just wiggled around!
The daisies whisper, 'What's taking so long?'
While ants march in sync to their tiny song.

I roll in the dirt; it feels like a spa,
With nature's own scents, and a close-up of stars!
The clouds above giggle as they float on by,
I wave up at them, and they wink an eye.

A pebble tells jokes; it's a real rocky pal,
While flowers play charades, is that a black snail?
In this lively patch, no reason to pout,
Just join the ensemble, let laughter ring out!

So here on the ground, we embrace with glee,
The joy of the world, all around, you see.
In earth's warm embrace, we dance and we twirl,
A whimsical life, oh how it does swirl!

Roots of Rejuvenation

I tripped on a root, what a sight!
My yoga pose left me in fright.
The tree just shrugged, said, 'Try again,'
While squirrels conspired, and I felt the strain.

I planted my face in the dirt, oh dear!
The worms cheered loudly, 'We're glad you're here!'
With grass tickling my nose, I made a vow,
To keep my dignity—someday, somehow.

A flower laughed, said, 'You need a hat!'
'Your hair's a nest for a stray alley cat.'
But with petals around me, I did not care,
For nature's my buddy, and I grew aware.

Now whenever I'm lost, I just close my eyes,
Imagining vines that stretch to the skies.
Roots wrap around me, in tangled embrace,
Turns out dirt is a cozy place!

Swaying with the Breeze

The wind whispered softly, 'Let's dance, oh come!'
As I twirled like a leaf, feeling quite numb.
A branch waved hello, and I gave a spin,
While ants judged my moves, with a sly little grin.

Grass blades applauded, swaying with glee,
'Your rhythm's impeccable, just look at me!'
I marched like a soldier, but stumbled a lot,
Even the daisies thought I had lost the plot.

A butterfly chuckled, flapping its wings,
'You call that a dance? You've got no strings!'
But I laughed with the trees as they rustled and swayed,
Who needs a dance floor when nature's your stage?

So here in the breeze, with no care in sight,
I twisted and spun till I felt just right.
And though I may trip over roots once again,
At least I've got friends, this green-hued realm's zen!

Verdant Reverie

I napped on a patch of bright, green grass,
Dreaming of gardens where fairies all sass.
They zipped all around with sparkles in tow,
'Let's sprinkle some magic, put on a show!'

A beetle called out, 'Join the pom-pom cheer!'
As daisies all danced, I could barely steer.
With petals like pom-poms, I joined the team,
But my moves were so clumsy, it ruined the dream.

The sun joined the party, shining so bright,
Saying, 'Dance like a dandelion, take flight!'
But I fell right over, wrapped in my grin,
While butterflies wondered if I'd ever win.

In the heart of the chaos, fun took its stand,
As nature threw blossoms, I waved my hand.
Laughter erupted—oh what a delight!
In this foolish reverie, everything's right!

Forest Symphony

The trees tapped their toes to the beat of the brook,
While I'm over here, trying not to look.
A chipmunk conducted with nuts in his hand,
Louder than any rock star in a funky band.

The mossy carpet mumbled with glee,
As crickets chirped out their symphony.
I joined in with claps, but missed the refrain,
Creating a racket like a runaway train.

A chorus of owls hooted in jest,
'Your rhythm's quite wild, we'll give you a rest!'
But with reeds as my mic, I sang out my song,
Encouraging bunnies to hop right along.

In this forest of laughter where melodies thrive,
I boogied and jived, feeling so alive.
So if you're ever lost, just dance with a tree,
Who knows what sweet symphony might set you free!

Healing in Hues

Underneath a bush so bright,
Laughter blooms by morning light.
Picking leaves with glee and cheer,
Nature's band, let's drink a beer!

Frogs in tuxedos play their tune,
Dancing 'neath the laughing moon.
Every flower tells a joke,
While squirrels give a silly poke.

The trees wear hats made out of moss,
And up above, a bird named Ross.
Tells tales of clouds that twist and turn,
With every step, our hearts will churn.

Life's a canvas, full of flair,
Brushes made of sun and air.
So let's paint with giggling glee,
With nature's quirks—just you and me!

Beneath the Canopy

Underneath the leafy dome,
Squirrels toss their acorns home.
With every rustle and a cheer,
I half expect to see a deer!

A chicken crossed the leafy path,
Claimed it found its hidden laugh.
Leaves whisper jokes like giggling maids,
While sunlight throws the funniest shades.

Jokes on the ants, so they conspire,
To build a tower even higher.
I join the fun, a leaf for a hat,
And dance with mosquitos, imagine that!

Under the sky, life's a playground,
With laughter echoing all around.
Join the shenanigans of this nutty scene,
Where nature's gags are purely keen!

Serenity in Bloom

Pansies prance with petals wide,
They giggle as the bees collide.
Dandelions throw a party near,
While butterflies bring snacks and cheer!

A rose confides the funniest tale,
Of thorny hugs that never fail.
Among the petals, jokes abound,
The fragrance laughs, it's beauty found.

In this garden of jest and fun,
Each flower shines, in every pun.
With worms that wiggle in a queue,
And ladybugs that pester too.

So come rejoice with nature's crew,
Where every hue is fresh and new.
With giggles woven in each thread,
A comedy show inside your head!

The Color of Renewal

In colors bright, we spin and twirl,
With brushstrokes bold, let laughter swirl.
An orange sock on a purple shoe,
Makes every walk a silly view!

Tulips tease the grand old oak,
"Join us, old friend, we crack a joke!"
Grass tickles toes with every tread,
While daisies whisper, "Just be fed!"

The painter's brush, a dolphin's leap,
Every stroke, a laugh, so deep.
With rainbows bright, we sing and swing,
In every hue, let laughter ring!

Rebirth in colors wild and free,
In nature's arms, just you and me.
Let's splash our smiles like fresh sunrise,
For humor's here, just take the prize!

Springs of Tranquility

In the park, the squirrels do dance,
Chasing tails in a playful trance.
With picnic ants in a tiny parade,
We laugh at the chaos they've made.

Beneath a tree, a dog gives a bark,
Chasing shadows that play in the dark.
A ladybug lands on a sandwich slice,
"Excuse me," it says, "but I'm feeling nice!"

A breeze comes by with a tickling shout,
As flowers bloom, the bees buzz about.
We join in the singsong of nature's jest,
Laughter is truly life's very best quest.

So grab your hats and find your cheer,
In vibrant parks, good moods are near.
With jolly jests and giggles supreme,
In a world of warmth, we bask and dream.

The Sound of Leaves

The leaves rustle with gossip today,
Whispering secrets as children play.
"Did you hear what the bug said to the tree?"
"Oh, do tell, I'm all ears, you see!"

Acorns scatter like tiny brown bombs,
Squirrels dive in with their cute little charms.
"Ouch!" one squeaks, right in the knee,
"Guess nature's trampoline is hard, whee-hee!"

Crisp leaves crunch beneath eager shoes,
The sound of laughter in every hue.
A bird lands near, wearing a frown,
"Trying to nap here, you silly town!"

But amidst all the fun and forest cheer,
We share smiles and grins, never a fear.
The joy of nature's silly embrace,
Brings giggles and joy to every face.

Blooming Serenity

Flowers bloom in a wacky parade,
Here comes a daisy, with a hat that it made.
"I'm dressed to impress," it bows with delight,
"Who's next for a twirl? Come join in the sight!"

Butterflies flutter, all colors in tow,
"Why did the bee wear a tux?" asked a crow.
"To impress the flower," chirped back a friend,
"Buzzing around until the very end!"

Sunshine giggles, painting all well,
On daisies and tulips, it weaves a spell.
"Oh, the world is a stage!" the gardener sings,
"Just wait for the blooms, oh, the joy that it brings!"

With playful whispers, we find our fun,
Nature's a canvas, oh, how we run!
In warmth and laughter, we all gather 'round,
For in this blooming, serenity's found.

Rebirth in the Wilderness

In the woods where the wild things roam,
A raccoon stumbles, looking for home.
"Hey, what's the fuss?" asks a wise old owl,
"Seems you're the king of the 'Oops' and the growl!"

The trees chuckle, their branches sway,
"Join us, dear friend, for a laugh today!"
Beneath their green caps, they share stories grand,
Of misadventures across this land.

A bear rolls by, with a snicker and grin,
"Why don't we take a stroll and spin?"
Through ferns and mud, they trudge on along,
Making up silly tunes, singing their song.

As twilight whispers with a soft silver light,
Creatures gather, all feeling just right.
In the wilderness, life's playful and bright,
Together we thrive, under the moonlight.

Harmonies of the Hearth

In the heart of my cozy room,
Where plants hum a gentle tune,
I found my cactus grinning wide,
As I sat down for a comfy ride.

The fern danced when I laughed out loud,
With each quirk, it was truly proud,
The pot had legs, yes, quite a sight,
Doing the cha-cha well into the night.

A spider plant in disco gear,
Spins around to bring some cheer,
While rubber trees tell funny tales,
Of mischievous squirrels and windy gales.

So bring your smile and take a seat,
Where every plant is a groovy beat,
Life's little quirks, we celebrate,
In this green space, isn't it great?

Petals of Peace

Upon the daisies, blooms have fun,
Making wishes under the sun,
Bumbling bees share giggles and buzz,
While flowers gossip, just because!

The violets claim they paint the skies,
With tiny brushes and crafty lies,
They mix up colors, oh what a blend,
In this garden where time won't end.

Tulips tiptoe in their finest shoes,
In a dance-off, none can refuse,
With petals whirling freely about,
They laugh at the clouds and dance with clout.

So come and laugh with the blooms so bright,
In this garden, everything feels right,
Each leaf a letter, each stem a rhyme,
Together we'll giggle, passing the time.

Roots of Contentment

Deep down where secrets are kept,
The roots wiggle and deftly crept,
Squirrels join in, teasing the soil,
With nutty jokes, they freely toiled.

The carrots wear a jaunty hat,
While peas insist they're quite the brat,
"Leaf me be, I'm just a sprout!"
They chuckle and frolic all about.

Underneath, they sketch a plan,
To form a band, yes indeed they can,
With potatoes tapping in the dark,
While garlic sings its own stark lark.

So lay down roots, let laughter flow,
In this underground talent show,
Where every giggle grows and blends,
In a pot of joy, where fun never ends.

Caress of the Breezes

Oh, how the breezes love to tease,
Whispers tickle the swaying trees,
Branches swaying, oh what a game,
Each leaf drops a joke, what a shame!

The sun beams in, says, "Hey, I'm here!"
While shadows mock with a chuckle so clear,
The grass tells tales of wild round-ups,
Where ants play cards and sip from tiny cups.

Petals flutter giggling in flight,
Dancing along with the soft moonlight,
Every breeze brings a funny tale,
From silly seeds to the gusts of hail.

So sway with the winds, take a cue,
Join in the laughter that swirls 'round you,
In nature's joke book, we find our glee,
In the caress of breezes, wild and free.

Treading on Thyme

I walked through the garden, oh what a sight,
Tripped on some herbs, gave me a fright.
The basil was laughing, the sage had a giggle,
I fell on the rosemary, what a strange wiggle!

The daisies were dancing, the weeds in a fuss,
I tickled a tulip, it said, "What's the rush?"
A snail offered advice, slow down, take a break,
But I just spun around, tripped over a rake!

I heard from the daisies, a secret so bold,
"We gather for parties, but never for gold!"
The peas in a pod were rolling with glee,
While carrots just chuckled, "That's just how we be!"

So if you're feeling heavy, or need a good chuckle,
Just waltz in the garden, and bring all your muckle.
The thyme will be waiting, with laughter and cheer,
In this curious world, you'll shed every fear!

Embracing Emerald

In a forest of folly, where ferns wear a grin,
I found my new buddies, with leaves that spin.
A parrot named Chuck flew down for a chat,
"Let's dance in the leaves, don't you dare sit flat!"

The moss hummed a tune, soft and so sly,
While the pines started clapping, oh my, oh my!
"Join us for laughter, the sun's shining bright,
It's a party of plants, every day, every night!"

A hedgehog played spoons, with mushrooms as drums,
While daisies in hats recruited more chums.
I took off my shoes, felt the grass on my toes,
With giggles and wiggles, the energy grows!

So come splash in the emerald, embrace the delight,
In the wild of the weeds, everything feels right.
Life's too short to hold onto sorrow and gloom,
Dance in the meadows, let laughter bloom!

Lush Reflections

In the mirror of nature, I saw something strange,
A frog doing yoga; oh how it could range!
With poses so awkward, yet filled with such grace,
I laughed so hard, fell flat on my face!

The willows were swaying, in rhythm so sweet,
Chatted with daisies, oh what a treat!
A squirrel told jokes about acorns and nuts,
And frogs always laughing, with their funny butts!

The river was gurgling, a serenade loud,
While pebbles were peeking, all hid in a crowd.
"What's that you say? Nature's odd but divine?"
"Embrace all the quirks, let your laughter entwine!"

So gaze at the lush, let its colors infuse,
With humor abundant, you've nothing to lose.
In leaves and reflections, find solace and glee,
Life's a joyous puddle, come jump in with me!

Solace Amongst the Shrubs

Strolled through the bushes, with giggles galore,
Met a fox who was knitting, from a thistle's spore.
"Need a cozy scarf for your chilly tail?"
"Only if it matches my berries on sale!"

The bees were all buzzing, performing a show,
Wearing little hats made of flower seed faux.
"Come join our fun, it's the buzz of the day!"
We tangled in petals, laughed all the way!

The hedges held meetings, discussing the rain,
"Do we really need water?" they pondered in vain.
"Oh please, not again! Just look at our greens!"
A grasshopper leaped in, bursting their scenes!

So find your own comfort, beneath leafy trees,
Join the quirky critters, just go with the breeze.
In this garden of solace, with laughter so loud,
Dance with the shrubs; you'll be nature's proud!

A Breath of Fresh Air

In the park, I take a stroll,
Where squirrels dance and birds console.
Leaves tickle my nose with joy,
As I dodge about like a little boy.

The wind plays tricks, it's quite a tease,
Whirling my hat like it's in a breeze.
A butterfly lands on my ear,
I laugh out loud, oh dear, oh dear!

Every step ignites a giggle,
At grasshoppers that leap and wiggle.
Nature's chaos, oh what a sight,
Turning frowns into pure delight!

So here's my secret, come and see,
Laughter blooms where the flowers be.
In nature's arms, we all should play,
For smiles chase grumpiness away!

Meadowland Musings

In a field where daisies grow,
I trip over my own big toe.
The bumblebees chuckle, oh so loud,
As I tumble down, not so proud.

Caterpillars in a race,
Slow and steady, what a pace!
I cheer them on with all my might,
While dandelions take to flight.

The sun starts to play peek-a-boo,
With shadows dancing all askew.
I join the fun, I spin around,
Laughing as I fall to the ground.

Amidst the green, I find my cheer,
With every giggle, there's no fear.
Embrace the whimsy of this place,
Nature's joy is the best embrace!

The Stillness of the Orchard

In the orchard, apples hang so low,
I reach for lunch, but missed, oh no!
A crafty squirrel laughs nearby,
As I ponder what to try.

The trees whisper secrets just for fun,
While I attempt to catch some sun.
I trip on roots, land with a thud,
Oops! Now I'm all covered in mud!

The pears look down, what a silly sight,
As I hop and skip from left to right.
Nature's laughter fills the air,
With every stumble, who needs care?

In this orchard, under the sun,
Life is a game, and I've just begun.
With fruits so ripe and smiles so wide,
In this whimsy, I take great pride!

Tides of the Terrene

At the creek, I dip my toes,
Splashing water, where it flows.
Frogs leap with a cheerful croak,
Their jumping skills? A funny joke!

The rocks giggle beneath the stream,
As I chase away my little dream.
A dragonfly zips to say hello,
But I'm too busy to stoop low.

The sun hitches a ride on the waves,
While fish dive deep, oh how they behave!
They tease like kids on a summer day,
In this watery world, we laugh and play.

So here's to splashes and silly cheers,
With nature's joy banishing fears.
In playful waters, our hearts convene,
Laughter flows like a silver sheen!

Calm Amongst the Foliage

In the leafy realm, I trip and slip,
Falling on a cabbage, what a comic flip!
Mice chuckle softly, hiding in the shade,
As I wrestle with a rogue, rebellious blade.

Butterflies tease me, flitting in the breeze,
While I do my dance, oh, won't you just see?
Grass tickles my toes, a mischievous friend,
In this wacky jungle, laughter can't end.

Dirt fights my shoes; they lose every time,
As plants giggle loud, they've a sense of rhyme.
Bees buzz around, stealing a light snack,
In this quirkiest place, we never hold back.

Oh, what a sight, under this leafy dome,
Finding joy in wild things, far away from home!
Who knew that the weeds could bring such delight,
In this cheerful jungle, everything feels right!

The Garden of Respite

In the garden's corner, I spotted a gnome,
Waving his hat, said, "Welcome to my home!"
He offered me daisies, quite a peculiar treat,
As the snails held a meeting, discussed their defeat.

The tomatoes were gossiping, juicy and bold,
Sharing their secrets, stories untold.
While cucumbers practiced their stand-up routine,
Laughter erupted, oh, what a scene!

Few weeds join the chat, trying to fit in,
But they crack a good joke about where they've been.
Even the carrots, proud in their rows,
Can't help but chuckle at the tales that they chose.

A party in petals, oh, what a delight!
Frolic and laughter, banish all fright.
In this strange patch, I just can't resist,
Celebrating with veggies, who'd ever guess this?

Serenity of the Wild

The squirrels perform tricks, they're quite the jest,
Jumping from branches, putting skills to the test.
While raccoons throw shade, sipping on dew,
Pondering life where the wild things brew.

A bear on a picnic has lost his cool,
Wrestling a sandwich, it's now a jewel.
The owls watch on, like judges in robes,
While lizards crack jokes in their green little globes.

Flowers in laughter, waving in the breeze,
Sharing their perfumes, making bees sneeze.
A fox tells a tale, one about cheese,
And all of nature feels eager to please.

As I lounge in the grasses, laughter resounds,
In this wild orchestra, humor abounds.
Who knew serenity hid twists so merry?
In the great outdoors, life's never too scary?

Petals of Peace

Petals sprout jokes, all in a bloom,
Sharing their laughter, dispelling all gloom.
A daisy said, "Pollen's a real heavy weight,"
While the sunflowers giggled, feeling so great.

In the pond, the lily pads gather for tea,
Chatting with frogs, oh, what a sight to see!
While turtles in hats recite silly rhymes,
And crickets play tunes, keeping up with the times.

A flock of bright birds joins in the fun,
With feathers a-flutter, they dance in the sun.
They chirp little songs, full of snickers and cheers,
While laughter and joy drown out all the fears.

As the moon peeks in, adorned with a grin,
The garden of jokes welcomes all to join in.
With petals of peace, we embrace the delight,
Who knew nature could play all day and night?

Walking in Vibrant Circles

I strolled through the park with a skipping delight,
Where squirrels did yoga, oh what a sight!
A dog wore a hat, as it chased its own tail,
While birds sang pop tunes, with a fresh, funny gale.

The trees waved their branches, grooving along,
With bushes that rustled in a dance, oh so strong.
Laughter erupted as I twirled 'round,
In this zany green world, joy tightly wound.

The flowers competed for best silly pose,
Winking and nodding, the petals all froze.
I tripped on a root, then burst out in glee,
Nature's a circus, come watch it with me!

As I pranced in the grass, the sun took its share,
Tickled my toes, didn't have a single care.
In vibrant circles, I found my new groove,
With chuckles and giggles, my spirit would move.

A Palette of Peace

With colors so bright, like a crayon box spree,
The daisies and dandelions danced happily.
I dipped my brush in the sky's azure hue,
And painted my worries away with a view.

The robins were artists, with worms in their beaks,
Creating bold masterpieces on sturdy old creeks.
I laughed as I watched them, their beaks in a frown,
Crafting their art, while I turned around.

The breeze brought me whispers of soft, leafy tunes,
As ants marched in line, wearing miniature spoons.
The sunbeams were giggling, tickling my nose,
In this canvas of chaos, pure happiness grows.

A palette of peace, where colors collide,
In nature's wild gallery, I take a fun ride.
Each brushstroke I make brings serenity's charm,
Laughing with petals, I feel their warm balm.

Blossoming Mindfulness

I sat in the meadow, a wise old fox grinned,
Telling me tales of where calmness begins.
He turned cartwheels and somersaults with flair,
While bees buzzed by, dancing without a care.

The daisies were talking, sharing their dreams,
Glad to spill secrets through their soft, sunny beams.
I joined in their chatter, with laughter so loud,
Sipping on sunshine, feeling quite proud.

A snail slid on by, moving slow as can be,
Screaming, "Life's not a race, just look at me!"
With every small moment, a chuckle I'd find,
In this field of reflections, I stayed in my mind.

With blossoms around me, I frolicked in cheer,
Joyfully learning that life's challenges steer.
Through giggles and whispers, my heart starts to leap,
As petals remind me, it's good to slow creep.

Scent of Healing Herbs

In the garden of giggles, plants whisper and sway,
With mint licking my toes, oh what a wild play!
Basil brought jokes, while thyme told a pun,
Their laughter was fragrant, under the warm sun.

Lemon balm giggled, all fresh and zesty,
It tickled my nose, made me feel so vest-y.
I danced with the rosemary, twirled with some sage,
Each herb becoming part of my humorous stage.

Chives chimed in with a chortle and cheer,
While lavender sighed, "Come plant yourself here!"
With every deep breath, I inhaled pure bliss,
The scents of this place I just couldn't resist.

In fields of aroma, I found smiles to share,
Nature's own remedy, beyond all compare.
With each little chuckle, I breathed in deep clove,
The healing of laughter, it's what I now love.

Seasons of Soothe

In springtime, flowers start to sneeze,
With pollen flying on the breeze.
A squirrel dances, a rabbit prances,
The birds all join in their funny romances.

Summer's here, let's play in shade,
An ice cream cone slowly made.
The bugs are buzzing, oh what a tune,
As I try to swat them with a spoon!

Autumn leaves make quite the mess,
Crunchy carpets can cause distress.
Yet running through, you might just trip,
And laugh as you fall, it's quite the slip!

Winter coats make us feel quite round,
Snowflakes twirl all over town.
Yet we build snowmen with grinning faces,
And throw snowballs in all the right places!

Mosaic of Moss

On stone and logs, bright green we see,
A fuzzy carpet, wild and free.
But stepping on it should be a sport,
You'll slip and giggle; what a report!

In rain, the moss gets nice and slick,
With every footstep, it plays a trick.
You can't resist a squishy bounce,
And suddenly, you're doing a flounce!

Sometimes it grows where you don't want,
Like in your shoes, oh what a haunt!
But squishing around, you find such fun,
As you hop and skip, until you're done!

A throne of green when you sit in peace,
Mossy pillows; your stress does cease.
In nature's arms, we snicker and chat,
Finding joy while wearing a hat!

Tranquil Tides of Turf

Waves of grass sway in the breeze,
With tiny critters—oh, what a tease!
Just try to sit and take a nap,
But ants will march, and there's no gap!

Kicking back on turf that's neat,
Grass blades tickle your little feet.
But watch out for the rollerblades,
Flying past like goofy parades!

Sometimes you'll find a soggy spot,
Where squishy mud is quite the plot.
You leap in joy, then face the fright,
Your shoes are gone! What a silly sight!

As day turns night, stars peek through,
Grasshoppers croak their nightly brew.
With every sound, you'll laugh and sigh,
Feeling lighter than clouds up high!

Echoing Elysium

In a meadow filled with vibrant sights,
   Chirping crickets host the nights.
With bright big frogs that leap so high,
   Who knew they'd sing with such a sly?

The breeze whispers secrets in my ear,
   While little deer prance without a fear.
   I try to whisper back, but oh dear!
I sound like a crow, what a weird career!

Butterflies float with patterns that pop,
   Dancing around, they just can't stop.
   But in their wake, I trip and fall,
   Land on my back; they giggle, I stall!

   Yet here in nature, laughter spills,
From joyful hearts to whimsical thrills.
   In this place, every moment shines,
   Nature's humor through the pines!

www.ingramcontent.com/pod-product-compliance
Lightning Source LLC
Chambersburg PA
CBHW072128070526
44585CB00016B/1584